Small Moon Curve

Small Moon Curve

Roz Goddard

Nine
Arches
Press

Small Moon Curve
Roz Goddard

ISBN: 978-1-913437-94-7
eISBN: 978-1-913437-95-4

First published July 2024 by:

Nine Arches Press
Unit 14, Sir Frank Whittle Business Centre,
Great Central Way, Rugby.
CV21 3XH
United Kingdom

www.ninearchespress.com

Printed on recycled paper in the United Kingdom by:
Imprint Digital

Nine Arches Press is supported using public funding
by Arts Council England.

Supported using public funding by
**ARTS COUNCIL
ENGLAND**

For Ian

Contents

Up late with Tess of the d'Urbervilles 11

'Why I danced and laughed only yesterday' 12

Sentinel 13

Carrying Tess 14

morning of the diagnosis 15

The dog-shaped key 16

In the Shrine Room 17

Stones, cold water (i) 18

Stones, cold water (ii) 19

In Root and Silt 20

Small Moon Curve 21

Scattering 22

Holding hands with Tess 23

Fattening field 24

Retreat (i) 25

In my hunger 26

Retreat (ii) 27

On Clent Hills 28

The late nineties 29

Singing with Frank Ifield 30

The Note 31

Talking to Mother Reborn in the Heaven 32
of the Thirty-three Gods

Some magic in my blood 33

All that is Silver and Ancient 34

My Father's Bathwater in a Kilner Jar 35

Three-cornered field 36

Times of Fury 37

Crow 38

The Ways I Carry You 39

Tenderness 40

Mr V wears a reindeer tie 41

Dreaming field 42

It's Time   43
I am soft and fear the hours   44
Two heartbeats spiking, falling away   46
Parakeets wake under a pink sky   47
All buds in April Swelling   48
Metta Bhavana for Tree   51
I want a stranger for Tess   52
Breast prosthesis as abandoned love   53
Breast prosthesis as sea creature   54
Song for Tess   55
Touch   56
Sweet peas   57
Bird app   58
Goldfish on the Coast   59
New Year's Eve Wedding Day   60
Walking with Ted   62

Notes and Acknowledgements   64

This opening to the life
we have refused
again and again
until now

– **David Whyte**

Up late with Tess of The d'Urbervilles

The winter I lost a breast,
I stayed awake watching oak
become a delta of dark rivers.

It will pass, this feeling of being
ripped in two. Morning comes
and light fills all the spaces.

I've been reading Tess.
She's driving the wagon
under sharp stars on the road

to Casterbridge, tired from
holding up the sky. It's the night
her horse is pierced by the mailcart.

Beehives scatter as glowing
lanterns along the drowsy lane.
I want to reach in and have her

lying next to me in the silence –
closing our fists tight, opening
them again, over and over –

until the bright pain
softens to the red tip of dawn.

'Why I danced and laughed only yesterday'

There's cancer there
we came out through
hushing doors

heavy in the new world,
carrying my small cluster
curled against winter.

A sunwheel caught.
on the car's bumper.
Christmas lights
shook on the pine.

Early stage –
a cool hand holding mine
in the shadows.

There were loved ones
waiting for news, for my name
to appear bright on a screen

but no mother
to scald a tea pot
murmur into my hair.

Sentinel

To lean into sky, feel its cradle
I walk out under trees half filled.
Danny the greyhound moves slow
carrying the world's sadness.
Aspen on high ground start up a sly song
'*What are you saying no to?*'
The doctor can't reach me in the woods
with her clarity like a shrine room-bell:
ductal   node   high grade
language for another woman's body.
Underfoot a sea of trip-root, needle
a call to earth through leaf fall.
Breast thrums. I stroke its snare skin
so full it could be milk coming in.

Carrying Tess

we walk the hill
of a dark holt
harebells down deep
by clay   slip into
wet ruts on the slope
lose our footing
in the gouged earth.
Tess never speaks
she's behind my eye
in her white dress
neither girl nor woman
fallen into my body
years ago as snow
or ipomoea's blue
opening.
I didn't know
you could carry
someone in your blood
as a shadow
or piece of silver.

morning of the diagnosis

a sparrowhawk takes a jay from
the garden. I'm standing in bare summer

stalks watching my life disappear.
I'm not the whole bird, parts of me

are filled with ice elsewhere
in the winter space.

The radio's tuned to a fat sun
where no-one's allowed to be sad

the presenter shines like polished glass.
the surgeon will see you at 10.00

please bring a partner or friend
I'm trying to breathe into terror

as I've been taught, under the fear
my heart is a tender breaking voice

you could lose all you love
I haven't been able to cry

even when I think of the surgeon
holding a thin folder of stars

light grading down to dark according to
histology, him washing his hands of me.

The dog-shaped key

Through the trees, sky is a wide
blue ocean inviting us to swim.
Park trembles with daffodils.
Spring arrived without frost,
magnolia's soprano section
dreams itself through a song.
Our dogs introduce us.
Yours drops a ball, mine claims it,
bounds away. We stand, our feet
in blossom, watching their game.
I had some bad news this morning,
I say, to you, to the birds, to
the unfathomable blue.
Mine drops the ball, yours picks up.
I'm sorry, you say. You're a stranger,
I need a stranger's ear. The dogs,
gentle agents, open a space
and we walk through: talk, murmur,
offer ourselves to each other.

In the Shrine Room

The Buddha's head is a crown of snails,
palm a landform at the mouth of a river.

I light candles, spark an incense stick
and kneel. This suit of armour is steel

stitched with strips of leather, bullet proof
against strife, daily revolts, duels

when I am called upon to draw a sword,
defend myself against insurgencies.

I ask that sorrow has breath enough
to be itself. Armour warms in the sun.

Under the breastplate, my heart is a wren's
small song. Take it from its bowl of ribs,

feel its gentle heat.

Stones, cold water (i)

On a women's retreat
in the valley of five hills

some of us swim at the river.
A woman dips to touch the bottom

brings up a shining stone –
we throw it between us

until someone misses the catch.
I sit on a rock in the shallows

net of summer dress billowing out
catching leaf, stick, tiny feathers.

Stones, cold water (ii)

A woman comments on the flow
and blue of it. The river is full of breasts

snow-light   ashen-blanched   pearly
later I walk back, past the old farmhouse

knickers sagging   one breast soused
head up the hill to a black reservoir

where pebble beaches appeared after drought
water low enough to see bones   what I must

find the courage to say are darting fish
in cold water.

There are stones in my marriage,
yellow as a sparrowhawk's stare.

In Root and Silt

Day ends late here   sits long in the forest
like a musing friend, *say more*

roams as a fire blessing the ridge.
Behind me a hollow, a square of oaks

where Tess lies between roots,
trampled heart hiccupping in the dark.

Small Moon Curve

Small moon curve, warm in my hand,
rising like a sweet bun. In another life

you would slip, wet with kisses from a silk
dress, sleep as a small animal through

a yellow afternoon. It's dawn.
Sunrise milks the skylight.

We're dressing in backless gowns,
ivory stockings. Oh, to hear a blackbird.

My wedding ring slides onto a finger of air.
The surgeon asks me to name my future.

You're performing a left breast mastectomy.
He touches my shoulder the way a bird lands,

feels ice under its feet, inks a cross near
the thickening. Each woman he visits sings her

own winter. We're a grove of tenderness as trees
in sorrow are. Two nurses walk me to theatre,

ask how I usually spend mornings. I mention
watching corvids, pot-bellied in oaks, listening

to their love songs from another realm.
I've lived the life of two crows.

Scattering

I show up to meditate
manage only more scattering.

Elephants anoint the wounds
of their beloved with dust.

I'm disappearing in my hospital bed
and the windows won't open.

My mother appears with a plate
of Welsh cakes.

This is how she spent her whole life
in a summer dress   invisible   bearing gifts.

Holding hands with Tess

River speaks a different language at midnight
loose tongued   intimate   a lover's hand in my hair.

You could drown your yearning here
the old horse is a god on the moonlit hill.

Small rain soaks our thin coats
warmth of the long day cradled in boughs

bats weave a sweet path over the field.
I'm holding hands with Tess, animals of the dark

wandering on   wounds fluttering with moths
the singing language of wind catches

in the crawl space of rocks   earth speaks
up through our feet: *listen, this is how.*

We are trained in deep sky work   know danger
when it's close   the day Tess meets Alec

a thick bass alarm sounds in her blood
red dust of Jupiter on her shoulders

what man forces strawberries into the mouth of a girl?

Fattening field

Alec grown unchecked
    the way a thicket
thorny and arching
     is a small world of dim light

keeping in the dead.

Plausible thicket
    its place tangled at the boundary
where small birds emerge –

summer's grace pours on fruits'
    sour hollows
grass snake sleeps
     roused by a girl's blush.

Retreat (i)

I watch a woman
walk through the long grass

of the farmer's field, on and on
into Welsh prairie country.

Ditches of black water
stretch for miles to the border,

her shoes are twins
on the stone wall.

In my hunger

Two weeks after mastectomy the surgeon
was known to remove bandages himself.
His hands passed through the air
with a pastry cook's delicate touch.
Beyond the hospital, after the immediate
trauma, hunger came. Foxes screamed
as I ate what was left in the fridge.
Blur of moon in frosted glass was not knowing.
Husband, have you noticed I'm a ravenous thing?
I wanted everyone. Including the surgeon who
liked to cycle in forests far from the city –
a Zen master in New Mexico, New Mexico itself,
the intermountain plateau, the plains.
I wanted to pass into space like a blown kiss.

Retreat (ii)

River gathers up its bed
burns roots along the bank.

When I walked the field late she'd
be staring at frozen waves of sunset

arms wide talking to the edge
of the world.

A white flag flew from her tent.
She appeared for afternoon meditation

carrying her shoes, soaked through
offered a star of wild garlic to the shrine

poured river into a white cup.

On Clent Hills

We're holding hands
husband and me

looking toward Wales.
The past stretches to a high ridge.

Rabbit shivers in long grass
stays still, waits for danger to pass.

Across the plain, hidden fires breathe up,
fields rule, the sugar factory sweetens the sky.

We talk about the sudden drop
where a mountain falls away

what we'll have for tea
anything but the ruby scar

across my chest. Holding hands.
The shame is distant smoke.

My rabbit heart falls asleep –
are we on a blighted star, Tess?

The late nineties

how I slept:
children each side
of the chimney breast

young in their beds
pigeons in the soot
lull of the universe

louder at night
and the house afloat
arms of the harbour wall

wrapped around our slick, gentle sea.
I slept through my mother's last call.
She spoke into the cave of the telephone

I can't get my breath.
By the time I played
the message back she was gone

covered in my father's gold
and all the things she never said
travelled loose as winged seeds.

When the gold was returned to me
it was the weight of a goose egg,
a palmful my father bargained for.

She wished to be better loved.
Her pendant: two butterflies
on the head of a sunflower.

Singing with Frank Ifield

We had a family picnic in the woods.
Mother was in love with Frank Ifield
    so smart, she said
and he could yodel –
I'm in love, I'm in love, I'm in love
with a wonderful guy!

She flew above us
in a kingdom of trees
releasing a voice
we'd never heard
like she was singing
the beginning
of the next universe –
love is coming.

The afternoon shades from certainty.
Did I wear a green dress?   Stone escarpment
rises beyond pines   honeyed in late sun

    we each took a corner of the blanket,
shook, as her entreaty to love got louder.

The Note

I slip the note into your coffin, feet end. My father
already scattered diamond rings across your chest
and now he is weeping in the corner. Aunts bring him
sweet things, bending to murmur in his ear as if he
is a child. I can't find you in my body. My chest all
electricity and heat, like a domino of pylons fell across
the English countryside and set the dry wheat alight
for miles. You are not there and I can't find you in my
belly either which is a vast cave where the wind has
dragged in crisp packets. I say all this in the note and
other things and imagine you smiling.

> *you are in the flame*
> *burn my finger as I reach*
> *twenty years of sighs*

Talking to Mother Reborn in the Heaven of the Thirty-three Gods

Mother, though you are pale, your lips
are hibiscus, full as the hem on a dancing
girl's skirt. Sun stitched into the narrow
pleats of your silk coat. Look at you now!
Your fingers, poised for music,
no trace of soil from the arc of calendulas
you planted behind the house.

The appraising stare is new, as if you see
my eyes shadowed with dust and wish
to thumb the ignorance away. There is a time
for silence, it is not now. I have made
this journey. Where are the thirty-three gods?
I imagined them silent in a cloister,
skulls bare to eternity, or quietly treading

heaven's mountainous paths. Are there
mountains up here? Do you jaunt off for afternoons?
Return worn out with apostle spoons and ask
for tea? You are different. Better dressed,
serene like those murmuring commandos
we encountered and mistook for novice monks.

You are keeping this heavenly knowledge
to yourself for now. I understand. It's starting
to rain. Soon this bower will be drenched
with the scent of bluebells. There is nothing
like seeing a person you love again, Mother.
The way it alters all things and makes the world
suddenly full of birdsong and yellow umbrellas.

Some magic in my blood

Tess has a world called Angel.
Love is love, warm as the side
of a cow she leans against.

when I saw him for the first time
my watering mouth

After her sorrows he's the burning light
of home.

neck as a new animal on his collar,
spread of honey on a white piece

To him she is misted with grace,
even her shoes seem holy.

I thought he must love the world
to reach out like that so gently
to the girl's sleeve –
touching fresh seas on a globe

When he learns her history, his faith
is a rain of needles in a bucket.

I was rooted in the bush as a songbird,
some magic in my blood set itself ticking

All that is Silver and Ancient

January, the month of shadows,
rooks rise from stripped branches,
catch themselves falling.

My father died in the coldest February.
Echiums stood as ghost pillars
as if fire had ripped through the neighbourhood.

*

This heart, even now swelling at the curvature of
the earth, the perfect milky edge of it, peeling away
forever as a road with no beginning or end, and
the sky beaming romantic and beckoning, offering
up its various blues and the universe literally on
my shoulders and all stars ready to drip light,
burn through to bone – fill me with all that is silver
and ancient. Even now, within touching distance
of God and the angels, the twenty-four Jinas and
lineage of saints, I wonder if you are scanning the
night imagining me as a small flare between the
constellations.

Nothing goes away.
Love settles in blood as sun.

My Father's Bathwater in a Kilner Jar

On cold days it clouds, a small fog
behind glass and you're back, smoking.

Are there panatellas where you are,
a back room to sit and watch the snow?

This water is precious to me:
mountain clear, grey, flat as the sea.

Do you still dream of crowning the 22 metre line,
of a gold cup for your roses in the county show?

I've heard frosts are hard, that clouds sparkle
and ring in the cold. Do you still sing?

Three-cornered field

sheep stand in autumn shadows
soft calling mounds
at the hedge,
    serried gulls reflected
in standing water

trees shiver red orange yellow
pull away, fall to ground

threading the needle
between truth and hope,
a letter spells out
Tess's grief as a knotted
thing with no room
to breathe.

She'll slide it under the door
to be read by candlelight
by Angel and his bruising god

Times of Fury

I've known the hum of grass
like a mother song, two of us
eating apples inside a hollow
yew, no world beyond
but hedges standing in heat
fields rolling from the hills
bringing song to our feet.
We're in a time after fury
weighted in glass beads
our faces partly snow –
dumb from the shock of what
we said. They're behind a barn
somewhere, those words
twitching in the grass.
We have only apples and soft
bread for the shock of what
we almost became.
My heart stands at the edge
of the pitch waiting to be called on,
bruising softened
to a poppy's dazed bow.
The village clock calls noon.

Crow

Tess, when the world narrows
to December's frozen leaf,
when our disagreement
is sorrow about the time
we have and how we should
love – I follow crow's
wing-beat to a high point
centuries old. We're shoulder
to shoulder in veils of frost.
His craw is full of days.
I lay food down.
He knows the world
passes in a train of hours
and he must keep flying.

The Ways I Carry You

Up ahead in yellow leaves
in daily bread, crow feed,
in plain cold glass as it tilts,
as it meets rain. As light collects
in the back seat of a lonely car,
when it's milk, when it spills.
In the space climbing stairs
where your body should be.

In half-awake morning saturation
from a dream
where we are prairie voles
in our bed of flattened moss.
In smoke and flames, in fingers,
when you are far away
and do not know
the ways I carry you.

Tenderness

Imagine the boat of yourself
in breaking light under willows:

a whole history waits
for the gentleness of rain.

On the foreshore of a different river
a woman finds a split coin in silt

conjures a realm from its gold rim.

Shame and vanity are patient as stone.
Hate wakes from a nap.

Everything calls for your tenderness
to turn toward it.

Mr V wears a reindeer tie

I concentrate on the hospital's curving sweeps,
      fresh fruit stall out front selling the red apples

of fairytales. A low building of secrets is wrapped
      in plastic. It's five days before Christmas.

My husband says everything will be alright.
      It's the time of masks, frosty roofs until noon,

winter's strange light stirred with treacle.
      At the sliding doors a palm tree is happiness.

We're shot with a temperature gun, nodded through,
      do the long walk past shady quads, head and heart,

lifts to acute and onto breasts. The surgeon will tell us
      if the cancer has spread, or whether my breast,

on its way to the stars, contained the high-grade cells
      within. We're called in. Mr V wears a reindeer tie, he's smiling.

Dreaming field

kitchen stone worn
         to moonshine

rainbows appear
         one upon another

Joan slides between
         cradle and range.

Suds and milk
         wreathe the room

in sweet mist
         stars pattern

on a sparkling sea
         weaving love

d'Urberville d'Urberville d'Urberville
         mother's spiral mantra

gilded possibility:
         Tess's high hat, aeons

of petticoats, riches
         awed whispers   elevation

plates of gold
         gleaming in the scullery

all troubles small
         cast into a raindrop

It's Time

Nature beckons a frightened girl
down the holloway

    past burned fields
to the hurst where bluebells

    are a sea of midwives
in violet bibs –

    the baby moves down,
down with the roots of elder,

    fat buds and their bronze tongues
poke into the world: it's time.

    A startled crow escapes,
Tess, braced against oak

    feels harvestmen push
beneath bark, the spark of furze

    is light – crossed fingers latch
deeper in earth, roots firm up ancient under fern.

She'll call her son Sorrow.

I am soft and fear the hours

During the maternity unit's
      longest night
the anaesthetist
      was called to a woman
who was ill
      and couldn't come
to my daughter's bed.

I wanted his skills for myself
      masked up
wheeling the steel trolley
      whistling, *sorry for the delay*

instruments laid out, each one able
      to land a perfect line
to a gentler level.

*

The bright corridors had an
atmosphere of negotiations
with white light – what we can't touch
or see but pray to –
behind each closed door a woman
on her own star
a child swimming inside her.

Nurses at their stations of bright screens
watching monitors for dips
accelerations, shrill bells of clamour –
the world outside, the coming dawn
can only be reached by crossing
a terrible sea.

*

I am soft and fear the hours
that I may be torn and no help to
my daughter. She's in a drugged sleep
contractions surge and collapse.
The midwife has told her to rest.
She'll start to push in an hour.

*

3.00 am shush of sliding doors
I walk into a night of muffled explosions.
Where are you in the black seamless sky,
fearlessness? Let it rain on my head –
a spell to shore up a scattered heart.

If I walk where sage has been, I trick time
and it's a safe July evening, I'm younger,
earth on the soles of my feet
eye to eye with an owl
dew soaking our feathers –
a bright planet covers a bench.

A woman, wrapped in a blanket
sits beside me, space station in free fall
her baby's not ready to come.

She's out for a breath of air
her boyfriend is playing cards
in another part of the city, 'joker'.
She refuses an oat cake
says we're a long way from the stars.
She'll call her daughter Celeste.

Two heartbeats spiking, falling away

Beyond a certain point
when the ocean stops breathing,
the consultant arrives with his team
like a constellation at the end of my daughter's bed.

I'm at her feet,
frozen in pre-dawn light.
The world shrunk to a galaxy
of monitors, two heartbeats
spiking, falling away
lub dub, lub dub –

concentrating on a piece
of cotton on the coverlet,
the consultant's blue collar.
Air is a fast river, it's wild
currents flow over us.
I know what it means
to ask for help, to kneel
with tight fists, and pray.

Parakeets wake under a pink sky

I see my grandson's head crowning
then retreating in the birth canal
'nearly here, darling;'
it will be a while before my heart
is a resting petal.

I'm back in theatre, 35 years ago, for the birth
of my daughter when I wanted to die –
death in my shoulders like a delicious weight.

We don't know yet that his fists
are either side of his face
muffling the beckoning calls
the urgent song of us.

*

He's born under a pink sky and the ballet of trucks
as men collect refuse in the hospital yard at dawn.

I have him in my arms,
his father wrapped him up

put his little white hat on. The 5:30 from
Los Angeles banks through broken cloud,

loose garlands of paraqueets flash green,
call out.

I talk quietly to him as he sleeps,
tell him about the people who already love him.

All Buds in April Swelling

i.m. Gareth Dyer, stillborn 2 August, 1956

Sweetheart, I call you, darling
        we're close as raindrops in a puddle.

It's all the same to us, the dissolving.
        You know my dreams:

northernmost at the edge of a lake
        where breath meets open water –

'are you loving the cold?'
        you want to know what I mean by sorrow

losing you, less ice
        your finger on joy, twist an apple

from its stalk, bite into sunset,
        show me the orchard's tender pocket

southerly on the black hill
        where cold air made a home

      *

Cypress swing on the roofline.
Pouring milk from a yellow jug
is an entreaty –
my hands on the apron leave
a whiff of lemon. Somewhere a dog lies
in the sun on blue tiles, a violin still warm
in the cool parlour.
This opening to love –
after six and a half decades brother,
I found you.

*

a newborn boy appears on my timeline
bowl of heat under a white cap
list pinned to a board –
pump, formula, wondersuit.
He's growing in the room of newspapers
cold tea, orange peel curled into a sigh.
His father, tender around the eyes –
a petal trader or colour merchant
smiles on – all buds in April swelling.
Alliums, a doubled field after the heat
of last summer, light from a tall window –
heartbeats as a spread wave.

*

My heart is water
(a frozen pail melts inch by inch)

everything new leaf
tansy, gentle sun

a double row of tulips
close enough for kissing

last night a robin sang in the cherry.
I understand nothing –

a little song, a leaf, a grain
of salt are unfathomable.

I'm sorry I didn't ask or say
his name, 'Gareth' one time

at the end of summer
standing in the warmth of things

or speak of the hour

the after-time. I'm living there.
It's Easter, Mom, pie cools on the sill.

I think of your loss
how it burned down the years.

Metta Bhavana for Tree

There are days I go
to the other talking world
in clay and silt

where truth is awake
underground, moving
through stem and leaf.

To what's-left-of-tree
living two lives
in its sucking henge –

narrow spruce
soft blade rising
at the edge-away –

difficult tree
maniac burrs
covering wounds.

To a grove of oaks
where I lean dissolving
under crowns of sugar.

All day, the sweet itch
where bugs found my skin.

I want a stranger for Tess

someone out walking,

delivering eggs, picking hedgerow
primroses for a kitchen vase,

pondering their own limitations.
A person liable to lift a fallen bird

from the path, feel pity for its clouded eye,
soft death weight, who will usher Tess

and her baby to a warm room
with blankets and an open window

through which spring air
will feel like protection.

Breast prosthesis as abandoned love

Before I sleep I think of your tread on a path
    of blossom as though we are floating.

Long-time here with paraphernalia
    from an old beauty routine – the touch of what's

forgotten and still exists. I laid warm over your heart,
    read it like a palm – your mother alive again,

singing, fists drilling wet sand, the wide billow of her
    skirt as a spaceship on the beach.

I dipped into your bowl of loves, testing colours with the lore
    of a dyer: sweet orange for tenderness, hawthorn's fierce leaf.

Winter's full moon whitened the moss that time
    we drove five hills in the dark, radio playing

More Love to Thee, O Christ, then a soft prayer,
    before you switched to the jazz station.

River nursed its silence as dawn came in –
    there'd never been so much light.

The snake road to Llanfoist was a drapery of rain
    as if we'd done something magnificent.

I'll settle warm as a clam in my cup, make a valley of us.
    The hours drip from a low roof into a darkening trough.

I miss how your walk was a slow dance.
    The way you listened like a tree.

Breast prosthesis as sea creature

a beautiful night in June, sea all swaying hips,
waves pour silver, bring eelgrass to adorn us.

You'll have seen us along the beach feeding in sand,
creatures glowing moonlight as women kayak

to the pier. We are alight, such beauty spread
along the strand. You've brought soft jazz,

perch a speaker on a rock, unroll your bed
of kelp, scoop a creature from its wet hole

stroke its nipple, tiny as a May bud,
blow to arouse the timid fire

pinch to make it blush.

Song for Tess

Song to garden dawned
in fading chorus
to blown rose, path
fox-licked dish

to foreboding
chased to an
egret stirring
at the edge of water

to Tess, heart pocket
flung wide to a bright
moment

song to lake hide
where we float
on a crown of weed,
to nine herons
looking east

seed as offering to the song
come wren, black cap, finch
song to trying again
in a light place

to frog blinking at the wood pile
to echium, written with sand,
reaching from its damp pot.

Touch

That first morning at the hospice
I hung out with the ambulance men
cracking jokes on the terrace.

We were on the sunny side,
a little club of the well with our
smiles and grand summer schemes.

Inside, I was afraid to step into
the circle where the dying sat,
serious gods with their own laws

and freight of terrible plans. As if in
their territory there was no love
or laughter or splashes of gin.

Months later when I'd grown up,
I held June's hand and found
her skin like mine, warm, craving touch.

Sweet peas

Each hot day strawberries
deepened their shining.
The dispute with neighbours
was over. Men came to cut
the high trees, a limewash
of fennel offered itself to the sky.
We lived in a sea of new light
grew sweet peas
birds flew by for the scent
the kitchen breathed July.
I left blooms trailing
over the fence
for neighbours to pick
hello, we've only got today. It's summer

Bird app

When the singing stops
there is no silence
simply marks on a grey beach
where the world lives on
listening to the forgotten –
don't pity me
everything has its life.

Goldfish on the Coast

How close we came to leaving each other
on the hard shoulder, walking in different
directions, following the line of fields
for lonely miles then hitching a lift –
me toward the sea, you with a spirit
level back to the midlands.

It would have been dark by the time
you put your key in the lock,
let yourself in to the cool hush;
prayer plants folded, landing light blown
and the dog staring into the night
expecting me to sing his name.

I'd have steadied myself on the coast,
bought a two-slot toaster, ruined a few heels
on the cobbles of the old town swaying home.
There would have been other men, a goldfish,
gulls screaming overhead, but no cause
for concern, none whatsoever.

New Year's Eve Wedding Day

It's New Year's Eve, Tess, mild as eggs.
I'm out early, close enough to a jay
to meet its cross-eyed stare.

A cock will crow out of place
in the high wind of late afternoon,
alert us to a sudden darkness.

Near water, a swan is still,
watching the long year sink into
horse chestnuts, passing leaves.

You are to be married today.
Your heart winters
in its burning hollow.

Should we tell our secrets, Tess,
live in the new ice age
foraging for berries?

Yesterday, at the florist, I picked out
yellow roses soft as tongues
fluting into the room like an early spring.

I made a party atmosphere:
lights winding the banister rail –
big paper stars hanging in clusters,

and dancing Tess, as we did in fields
when we were young, our dresses
larking about us with lives of their own.

We're at year's end –
our throats a craw of snakes,
there is yet time for our secrets

to lie awhile. Forgiveness is quiet
under the raging water of the falls.
Let us forgive ourselves and swim.

Walking with Ted

Aquilegia's tender clover
sticks of winter, pink in late sun –

we walk the frosted lawn,
pass a snail shell palm to palm.

Tiny blossoms, a white stone,
are small gifts between us.

You drop my hand, fall softly,
as if you are full of sweet apples

about to discover grass. Grandson,
you return the world's beauty –

city glows under a trembling sun
a mandala of rooks shine –

loosen like sand to the edge of cloud –
I see it all for the first time.

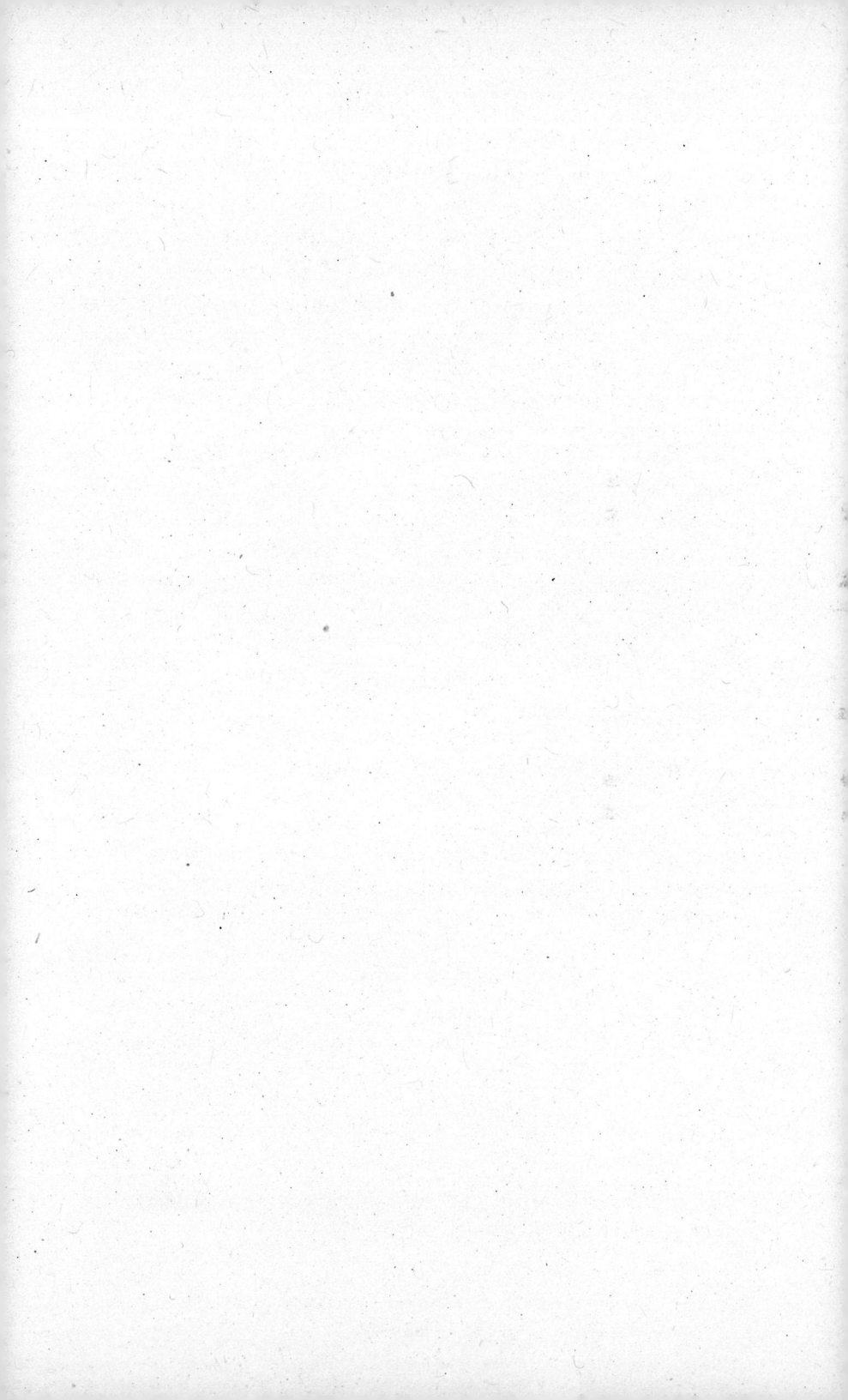

Notes and Acknowledgements

After my diagnosis, treatment and recovery from breast cancer during the winter of 2020/21, I drew on many things to help me come to terms with my illness. My husband Ian and my children Rose and Ewan and friends in the Buddhist Sangha were a huge source of love and support during this difficult time, for which I am deeply grateful. My faith and its emphasis on meditation and drawing closer to one's pain as a way of cultivating acceptance and compassion for oneself was vital.

There was also a sleeping presence in my blood who took me by surprise. I'd read Thomas Hardy's *Tess of the d'Urbervilles* as a teenager and had long found Tess to be a deeply compelling character. The loss and heartbreak she endured stayed with me over the decades. Her fortitude, independence and spirit too. She emerged strongly in the darkness of my winter illness, as a companion, guide and inspiration.

My source text was: Thomas Hardy, *Tess of the d'Urbervilles*, Penguin Classics, 1998.

The field names I invented and used for scenes involving Tess were inspired by: *meathfieldnames.com*

Background reading on crows came from: *Franklin Coombs, The Crows: A study of the Corvids of Europe, 1978, pub: B.T. Batsford Ltd*

*

Thanks are due to the editors in which the following work appeared and to The Ledbury Poetry Festival for the 2017 commission.

The poem 'Talking to Mother Reborn in the Heaven of the Thirty-three Gods' was commissioned for The Enemies Project at the Ledbury Poetry Festival, 2017 and first appeared in a pamphlet, *Spill*, pub by Flarestack Poets in 2018.

'Touch', which was shortlisted for the Bridport Prize in 2014, 'The Ways I Carry you', 'Goldfish on the Coast', 'In the Shrine Room' and a version of 'My Father's Bathwater in a Kilner Jar' appeared in *Spill*, as above.

'Sentinel' and Mr V wears a reindeer tie' appeared in *Poetry Birmingham*, Issue 7, Autumn/Winter 2021.

'morning of the diagnosis', was published in *Bad Lilies* Issue Six: Private Universe, in February 2022.

'Small Moon Curve' was a finalist in *The Moth* Poetry Prize 2021 and appeared in *The Moth* magazine in Issue 48, Spring 2022.

'The dog-shaped key' was commissioned by Poetry on Loan.

I am hugely grateful to my editor, Jane Commane of Nine Arches Press, for her gentle and forensic editing and to Jonathan Davidson and Liz Berry for their comments, questions and advice which helped to sharpen and focus the manuscript.